LA PIRE DES PRINCESSES

Pour Guinevere, Niamh, Emelia, Esther, Elise, Esme, Martha, Orla
et toutes les princesses rebelles du monde – A. K.
Pour Freya et Molly – S. O.

Première édition : © 2012 par Simon and Schuster UK Ltd, Royaume-Uni, sous le titre *The Worst Princess*.

1, rond-point du Général-Eisenhower, 31101 Toulouse Cedex 9, France.

Loi 49.956 du 16 juillet 1949 sur les publications destinées à la jeunesse.
Dépôt légal : 2e trimestre 2013.
ISBN : 978-2-7459-6209-6.
Achevé d'imprimer au 2e trimestre 2019 en Chine.
editionsmilan.com

LA PIRE DES PRINCESSES

ANNA KEMP ◆ SARA OGILVIE

Adaptation française d'Emmanuelle Pingault

MILAN

Il était une fois, tout près d'ici,
une princesse nommée Zélie.

« On dit qu'un jour mon prince viendra...
mais ça fait cent ans que je l'attends !

Je n'en peux plus, qu'il se dépêche,
qu'il bouge un peu ses royales fesses !

J'ai lu tous les contes de fées,
je pourrais même les réciter.
Mes nattes n'en finissent
plus de pousser, j'ai grand besoin
de m'aérer, voir le monde,
changer de tête et d'univers ! »

Mais alors qu'elle se lamente...

… soudain paraît à l'horizon
un magnifique cavalier
chevauchant son fier destrier :
« Douce princesse aux longues tresses,
j'ai tant trotté pour te trouver !

D'une main sûre j'ai lutté,

j'ai affronté mille dangers.

J'ai tranché vifs à coups de glaive
ceux qui m'éloignaient de mon rêve.

– Trop bien, dit Zélie. On y va ?
Mais, d'abord, un baiser.
Approche, je vais te montrer ! »

Sitôt sur le cheval fringant,
Zélie rit : « Youpi ! En avant !
Tout est bien qui commence bien ! »

Mais que voit-elle au premier virage ?

« Où allons-nous, prince charmant ?
– Dans mon château, ma belle enfant,
mon fruit sucré, mon potiron ;
ta chambre est là, dans le donjon.

– Mais, moi, je préfère chevaucher, sortir, découvrir, explorer ! »

Le prince rétorque :
« Dommage, ma chère, car tout ça
n'est pas au programme.

Tu devrais le savoir : c'est moi qui porte
l'armure ; toi, tu ne manques pas de robes...

Ici, c'est moi l'aventurier.
Contente-toi de soupirer,
de saluer ton prince intrépide
d'un sourire gracieux et timide. »

Seule dans le donjon, Zélie moisit :
« Charmant, mon prince ? Plutôt crétin !
Mais que vois-je luire à l'horizon ?

Les yeux de braise d'un dragon ! »

Loin de trembler, Zélie sourit :
elle a une idée de génie.

« Hé, toi, crie-t-elle, vilain griffu !
Tu veux du thé ? J'ai pas tout bu !
– Oh oui, merci ! J'ai la vie dure
à cause d'un grand fou en armure.

– Et moi donc ! Ce vieil arriéré
m'a enfermée dans son palais.

– L'affreux goujat ! rugit le monstre. Cela ne saurait durer. On va lui donner une leçon ! Une petite pulvérisation… »

Et, d'un souffle, il détruit la tour !

Le prince en est scandalisé :
« Ma dulcinée, c'est insensé !
Ta robe est déchiquetée, ma tour en miettes !
Tu es la pire des princesses !

Enfin, et c'est un lourd grief,
un dragon squatte dans mon fief !

– Tu l'as dit : je suis négligée,
hérissée et mal fagotée. Et alors ?
C'est décidé, je prends la porte.
Et que le dragon m'emporte ! »

Sans redouter un coup d'épée,
le dragon n'a qu'à éternuer.

Houla, ça sent le brûlé !

Depuis ce jour, les deux complices parcourent ensemble les contrées.

Et parfois ils ne résistent pas…

... à griller quelques princes crétins
ou chevaliers hautains.

« Être princesse, c'est un métier !
Cloîtrées dans leur placard doré,
certaines font de la manucure ;
moi, je veux vivre d'aventure. »

Ils vécurent heureux pour toujours !

LILY & LUCA'S
ADVENTURE
AT
THE CAVE

Lily & Luca's Adventure at the Cave

Published in Barbados by GABCEY Productions

ISBN 978-976-96534-0-5

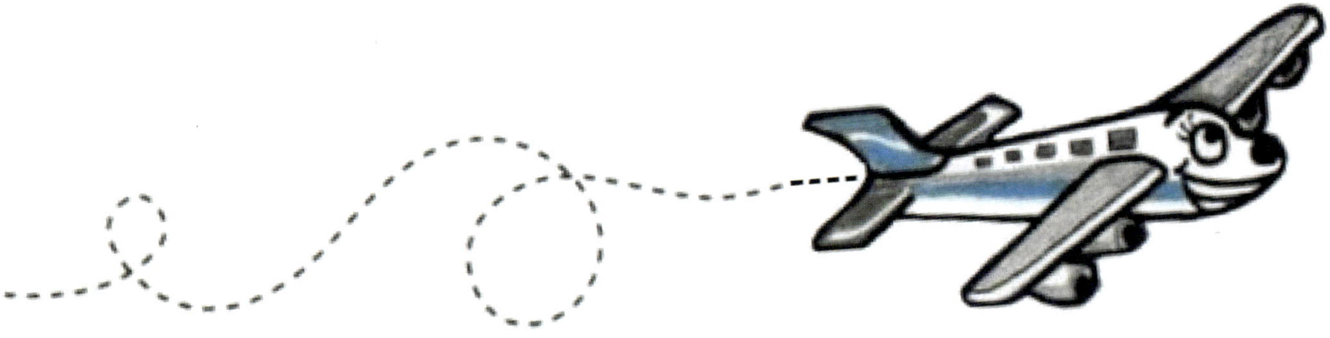

FUN ACTIVITIES TO DO

- Cave Word Scramble
- Cave Maze
- Colour the Formations
- Cave Word Search
- Name The Animals & Insects
- Secret Code
- Colour the Guide
- Cave Crossword Puzzle
- Cave Quiz

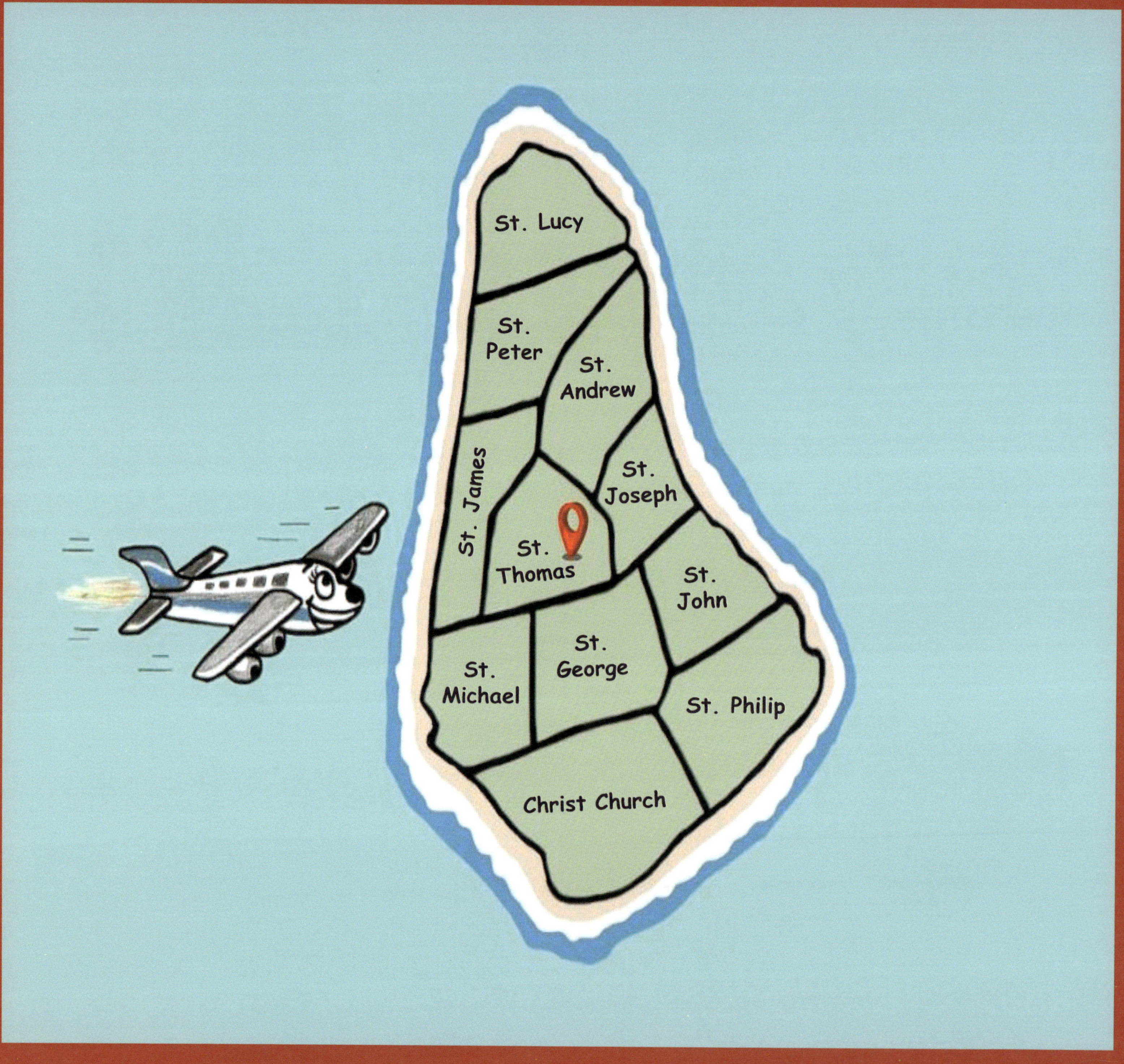
St. Lucy
St. Peter
St. Andrew
St. James
St. Joseph
St. Thomas
St. John
St. Michael
St. George
St. Philip
Christ Church

Lily and Luca are eleven year old twins who live in Yorkshire, England.

They are very close and enjoy doing lots of things together.

Their grandparents were born in Barbados, so last summer their parents took them on a trip to the island.

It was a dream come true. They travelled to a faraway country for the first time.

In Barbados, Lily and Luca did lots of fun things.
They went to the beach, ate local food and visited exciting places.

During the last week of their holiday, Lily and Luca toured a gigantic cave, considered as a unique tourist attraction.

Upon arrival, the family paid and received tickets for the tram tour.

They used the elevator and
arrived at the visitors' centre.

Cave Word Scramble

Unscramble the letters to make a word!

1. evlatroe ___ ___ ___ ___ ___ ___ ___ ___

2. truo ___ ___ ___ ___

3. andvuteer ___ ___ ___ ___ ___ ___ ___ ___ ___

4. vsiotir ___ ___ ___ ___ ___ ___ ___

5. rkoc ___ ___ ___ ___

6. wdneor ___ ___ ___ ___ ___ ___

7. dsciovre ___ ___ ___ ___ ___ ___ ___ ___

8. hystrio ___ ___ ___ ___ ___ ___ ___

9. gidue ___ ___ ___ ___ ___

10. ploso ___ ___ ___ ___ ___

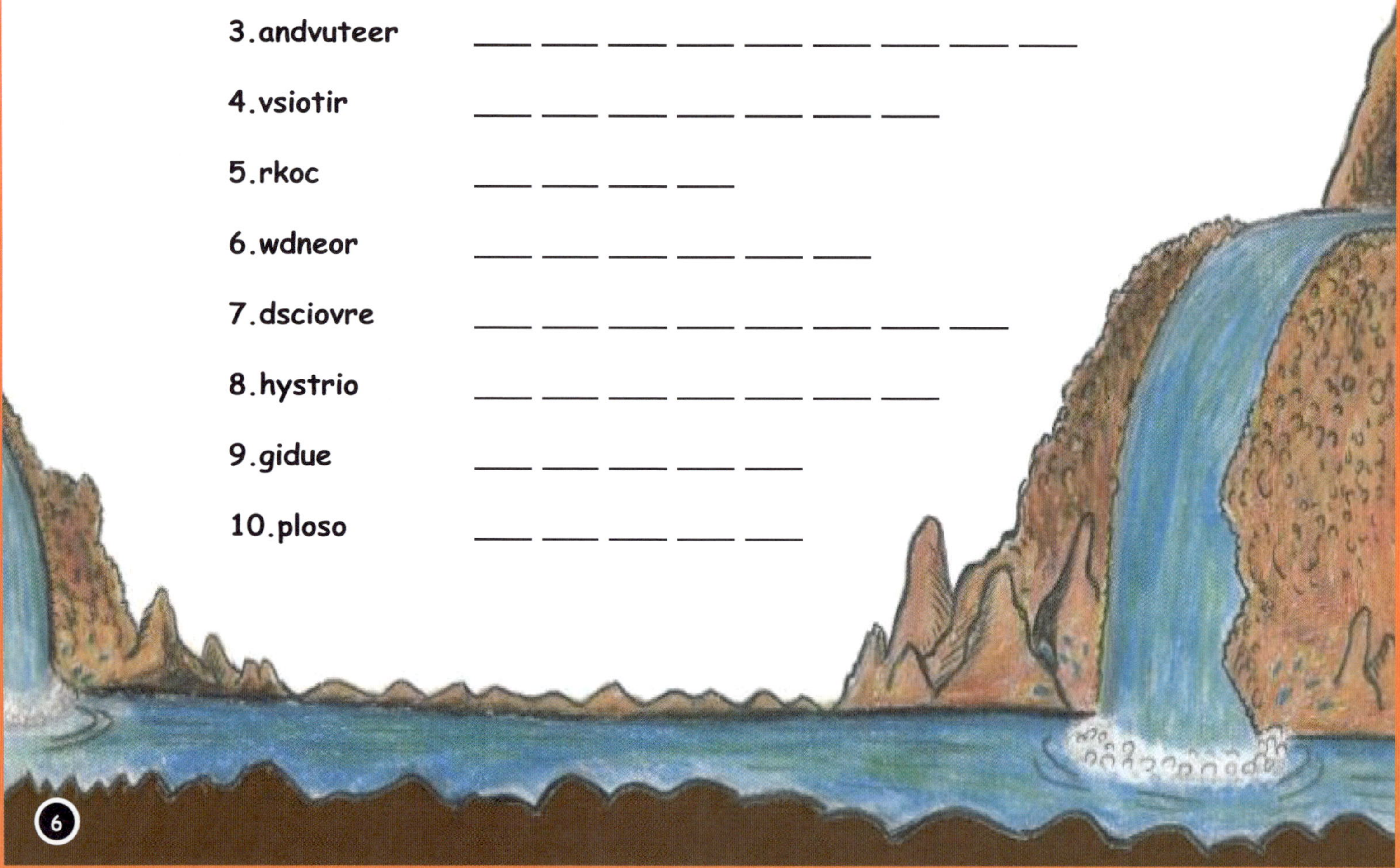

In the visitors' centre they were greeted by a friendly tour guide named Christine.

Before the start of the tour, they watched a short and interesting movie on the discovery and formation of the cave.

❑ It is located in the parish of St. Thomas.

❑ It is named after a man called Thomas Harrison.

❑ It is situated 700 feet above sea level.

❑ It is made of coral and limestone.

❑ It was opened to the public in 1981.

❑ It is a natural wonder.

❑ It is an ecosystem - an environment where living organisms depend on each other to survive.

Cave Maze

Help Luca get what he needs for the tour!

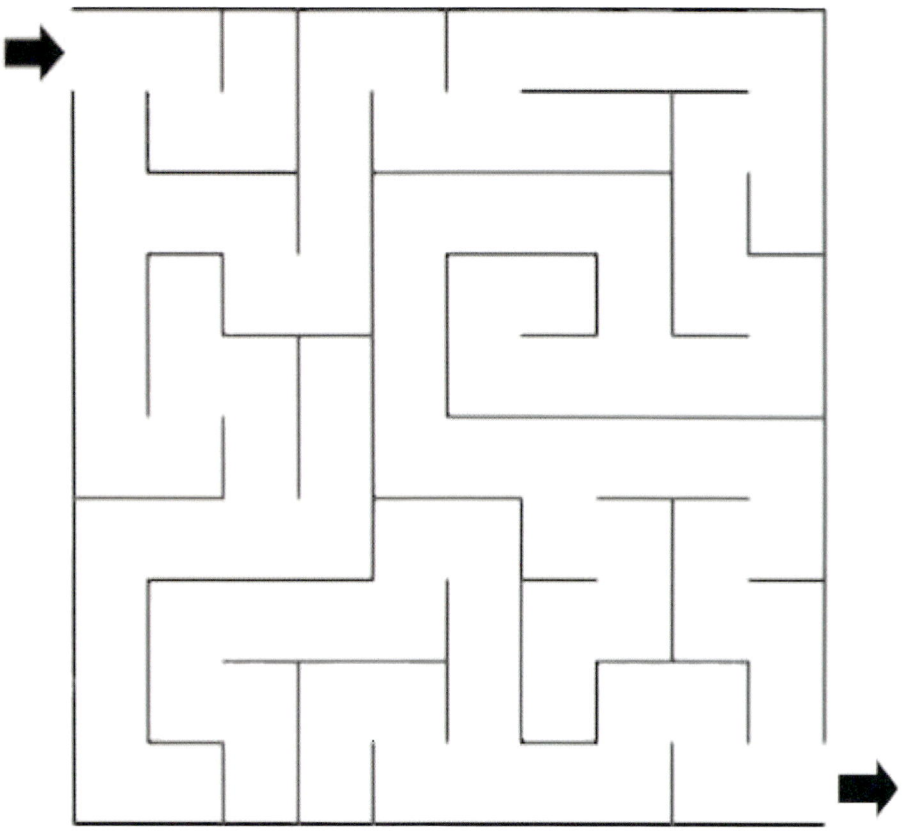

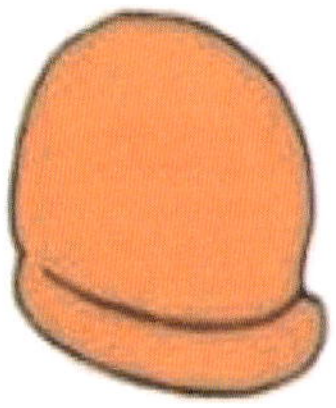

After everyone had covered their heads with hardhats,
it was time to begin the great adventure.

The lights in the cave made it easy for them to see the beautiful stalactites and stalagmites.

They learnt that stalactites hang downwards from the cave ceiling and stalagmites grow upwards from the cave floor.

The journey underground was breathtaking.

Colour the Formations!
Stalactites = Yellow
Stalagmites = Orange

The tram stopped for them to get a closer look at the rock formations.

Christine was happy to take a photo of the children in front of a small waterfall.

During the tour, the lights were turned off and they experienced the natural darkness of the cave.

Suddenly, a spotlight appeared on a couple who were on a private tour.

To everyone's amazement the man got down on one knee and proposed to his girlfriend.

Cave Word Search

Y	L	A	S	Y	N	M	O	B	S	G	W	O
L	I	H	E	E	O	A	U	A	T	L	X	S
L	M	I	T	N	I	R	W	R	R	B	J	E
U	E	S	I	R	T	T	D	B	E	F	W	T
G	S	T	T	U	C	P	U	A	A	U	Z	I
X	T	O	C	O	A	E	X	D	M	U	D	M
P	O	R	A	J	R	L	A	O	S	I	W	G
O	N	Y	L	M	T	X	I	S	P	J	M	A
G	E	J	A	P	T	P	H	O	T	O	S	L
J	G	P	T	J	A	T	U	N	N	E	L	A
X	D	N	S	E	R	O	L	P	X	E	E	T
E	R	U	T	A	R	E	P	M	E	T	U	S
U	N	D	E	R	G	R	O	U	N	D	T	A

Find the words from the list!

ATTRACTION
BARBADOS
EXPLORE
GULLY
HISTORY
JOURNEY
LIMESTONE
PHOTOS
STALACTITES
STALAGMITES
STREAMS
TEMPERATURE
TRAM
TUNNEL
UNDERGROUND

Along the way on the tour, they saw a small group of people
in the water climbing a ladder.

Christine said they were on an adventure tour.

It seemed like a lot of fun, and Christine encouraged everyone to come back and try that tour.

Christine described the animals and insects that can be found in the cave.

Luca was curious about bats and hoped to see one up close.

Name the Animals & Insects

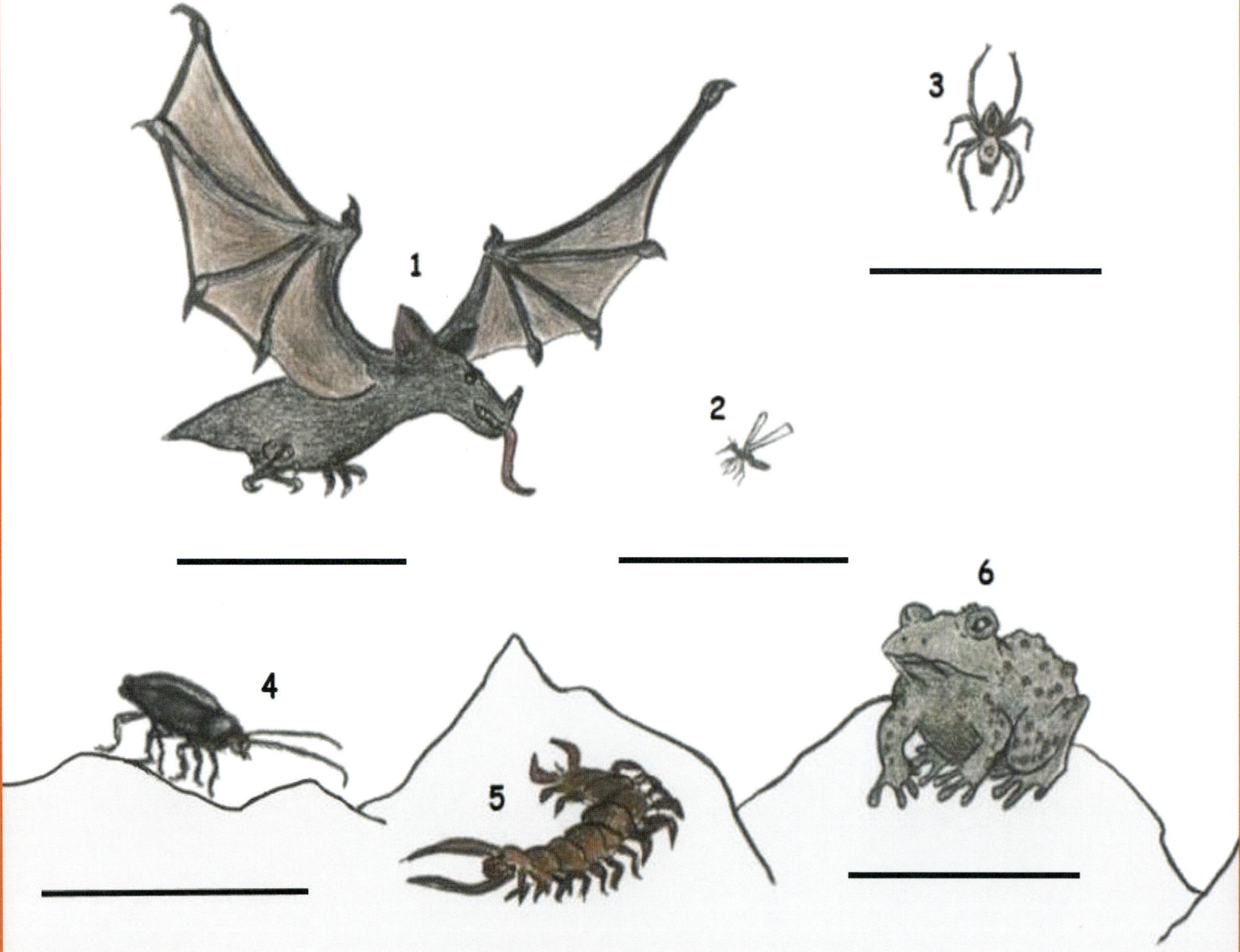

The tour underground was wonderful with a pleasant driver and a knowledgeable guide.

Secret Code

Lily and Luca left their tour guide a message in secret code, but she has no idea what it says. Can you help her out?

___ ___ ___ ___ ___   ___ ___ ___
2 11 1 7 5   10 6 8

___ ___ ___   ___
14 6 9   1

___ ___ ___ ___ ___   ___ ___ ___ ___
15 9 13 1 2   2 6 8 9

___ ___ ___ ___ ___ ___ ___ ___ ___!
4 11 9 12 3 2 12 7 13

1=A	2=T	3=S	4=C	5=K
6=O	7=N	8=U	9=R	10=Y
11=H	12=I	13=E	14=F	15=G

Colour The Guide That Is Different!

Outside the visitors' centre, the family walked around admiring the beautiful scenery filled with exotic plants.

Suddenly, they spotted green monkeys in a tree.

Luca showed Lily a mother monkey protecting her infant.

Cave Crossword Puzzle

Fill the boxes with the answers that fit each clue!

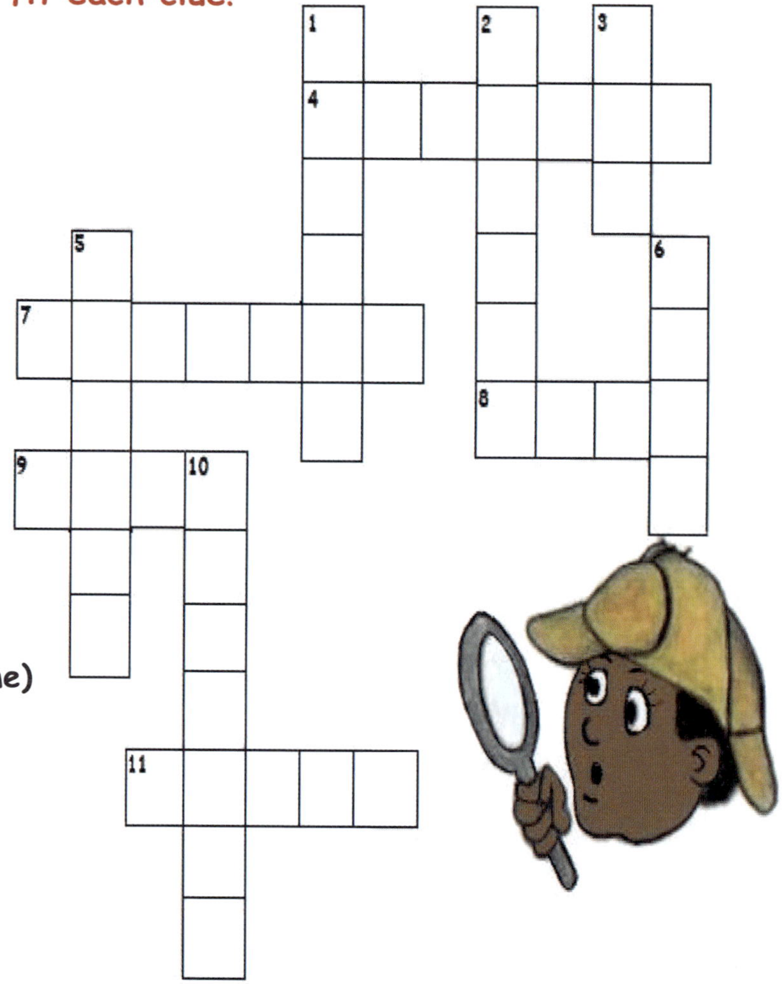

ACROSS

4. Similar in meaning to vacation
7. Something you cover your head with
8. To visit a place for sightseeing
9. A large underground hole
11. A motion picture

DOWN

1. The cave was named after him **(first name)**
2. Pay and receive this
3. It lives in the cave
5. What monkeys like to eat
6. The cave is naturally __ __ __ __
10. To search and discover new things

After a very exciting tour and a quick stop at the Cave's gift shop,
Lily and Luca decided to race each other back to the car.

As they drove off Lily and Luca
remembered the wonderful
things that
they had seen.

It was an adventure that they
would never forget!

Cave Quiz

Put a check mark next to the correct answer!

1. Where is the Cave located?

   ☐ St. Lucy ☐ St. Philip ☐ St. Thomas

2. What year did the Cave open to the public?

   ☐ 1966 ☐ 1981 ☐ 1995

3. The Cave is man-made. ☐ True ☐ False

4. The Cave is NOT made of

   ☐ Limestone ☐ Plastic ☐ Coral

5. Visitors travel through the Cave by

   ☐ Tram ☐ Bicycle ☐ Car

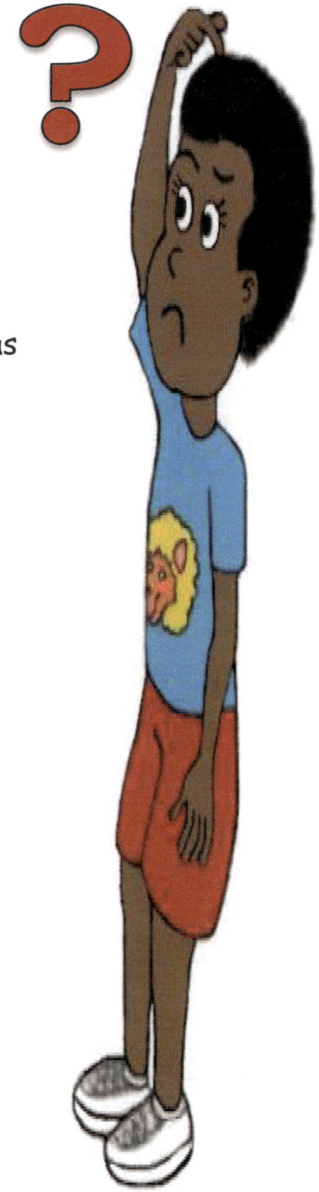

Lily and Luca really enjoyed their time in Barbados and could only think about their next visit, hopefully soon!

We took pleasure in creating this illustrated book and would like to offer thanks to a number of people.

- God, for the ability to create and complete this book.

- Mrs. Margo Clarke and Ms. Sonja Welch, GCM, for taking the time to proof read our book.

- Pastor Noel Jordan Th.D., D.D., D. Min and Pastor Annette Jordan Th.D., D.D., D. Min, for their continual prayers and support.

- All persons who support local talent, which enables us to continue creating educational and enjoyable children's literature.

Answers to Worksheets

- **Cave Word Scramble**

  1. elevator 2. tour 3. adventure 4. visitor 5. rock
  6. wonder 7. discover 8. history 9. guide 10. pools

- **Name the Animals and Insects**

  1. bat 2. mosquito 3. spider 4. cockroach 5. centipede 6. toad

- **Secret Code**

  THANK YOU FOR A GREAT TOUR CHRISTINE

- **Cave Crossword Puzzle**

  Across 4. Holiday 7. Hardhat 8. Tour 9. Cave 11. Movie
  Down 1. Thomas 2. Ticket 3. Bat 5. Banana 6. Dark 10. Explore

- **Cave Quiz**

  1. St. Thomas 2. 1981 3. False 4. Plastic 5. Tram